Royal Family Library

Her Majesty
The Queen

CRESCENT – New York

Introduction

On her twenty-first birthday Princess Elizabeth broadcast a radio message from South Africa where she was on an official tour with her parents. In it, she declared that she dedicated her whole life to the service of her country. Since that day she has not faltered in her task.

When a daughter, Elizabeth Alexandra Mary, was born to the Duke and Duchess of York at their London home, 17 Bruton Street, on 21st April 1926 no one imagined that she would one day become Queen of England.

The Princess, whose father was second in line to the throne, lived quietly with her parents and younger sister Margaret Rose until, in 1935, her grandfather King George V died. For a while life went on as normal, but in 1936 her uncle Edward VIII abdicated and her father became King of England. The ten-year-old Princess was then Heiress-Presumptive to the throne.

With her parents, Princess Elizabeth moved into Buckingham Palace and soon began learning the difficult lessons of monarchy. She was educated privately, but extensively, concentrating on history and languages as well as other subjects. In London she visited the Tower and other historic places and museums, and gradually began to take part in official functions with her parents. When the Second World War broke out in 1939, she and Princess Margaret were sent to Windsor Castle as a safety measure while their parents remained in London.

The young Princess played her part in helping the people of wartime Britain by knitting, collecting things for the war effort, and being an active member of the Girl Guides. She broadcast a message to the children of Britain, and in 1945, when she was eighteen, she joined the ATS as a junior subaltern in the mechanised transport corps becoming proficient as a motor mechanic and driver. She is still an excellent driver today, but drives herself only when she is on her estates.

In the first years of peace after the War she accompanied her parents on their tour of South Africa. It was here that she made her historic broadcast on her twenty-first birthday. After returning to England she became engaged to Lieutenant Philip Mountbatten RN and they were married at Westminster Abbey in November 1947. Her husband was created Duke of Edinburgh by Princess Elizabeth's father, the King. In 1948 their first child, Prince Charles, was born, followed by Princess Anne in 1950, and the Princes Andrew and Edward in 1960 and 1964.

In 1952, during a tour of Kenya, the King died and Princess Elizabeth returned home immediately to take up the onerous task of Queen of England. She was crowned in Westminster Abbey in June 1953. During the reign of her father, many countries in the former British Empire were given their independence but many remained as members of the Commonwealth of which the Queen is head. On the eve of her Coronation she learned that a British team, led by Sir John Hunt, had conquered Mount Everest. People throughout the land rejoiced at this great achievement of the team, especially two of its members – the New Zealander Sir Edmund Hillary and Sherpa Tensing.

She is the first Queen to have had her Coronation service televised and watched by millions of people all over the world. She was also the first to ride on horseback at the head of her troops since the reign of Queen Elizabeth I four hundred years earlier. Later Queens preferred to ride in the more sedate carriages when taking the salute at the Queen's Birthday Parade or Trooping the Colour Ceremony in June each year. In 1957, she was the first Queen of England to televise her annual Christmas broadcast. These radio broadcasts had been instituted by her grandfather, King George V. In 1969, she gave permission for a royal documentary of a year in the lives of her family to be made and shown on television. *Royal Family,* as it was called, was an immediate success. It opened the secret world of the monarchy to millions of people and showed how much work and planning goes into the busy life of the Queen and her family. The Queen is the most travelled monarch in the modern-day world and each year undertakes foreign tours, sometimes travelling very long distances. In 1977, the Jubilee Year, one such tour to New Zealand, Australia and New Guinea covered about 50,000 kilometres in nearly fifty separate flights.

A clear pattern of the Queen's life gradually emerged over the years. Her programme has included annual events, as well as extra duties such as the royal tours overseas for which there is much planning and preparation, the reciprocal visits of Heads of State and dignitaries to England and Royal visits to all parts of the British Isles. In 1972, she enjoyed the personal joy of her own Silver Wedding with a special Service of Thanksgiving in St Paul's Cathedral and Luncheon at the Guildhall.

The climax of her reign, the Silver Jubilee celebrating twenty-five years on the throne, came in 1977. It was a year to remember. The Queen undertook a tour of the Commonwealth and most parts of the United Kingdom, including Northern Ireland, must have been greatly encouraged by the enthusiasm and interest shown by people everywhere.

The Queen is an indefatigable woman who is steadfast to her task and carries out her duties with dedication. Throughout her reign she has been supported by the love of her family, an obvious source of strength to her. After her Coronation in 1953 the late Sir Winston Churchill spoke the following words: 'We have had a day which the old are proud to have lived to see and which the youngest will remember all their lives'. Indeed those words could be applied to her entire reign and her example and service are still something to be proud of in the busy decade of the eighties. Long may she reign!

Early Life

Princess Elizabeth, elder daughter of King George VI and Queen Elizabeth enjoyed her childhood, especially time spent with the family in the country at Windsor, Sandringham or in Scotland. She shared her parents' love for Balmoral where she was able to relax away from the cares of State and public life.

On her father's accession to the throne in 1936, her official training for monarchy began in earnest. To mark her sixteenth birthday, in 1942, she was given her first official appointment as honorary Colonel of the Grenadier Guards. She took the salute at a special march past and birthday parade and proudly wore their badge in her military style hat. Like other girls of her age she registered for National Service, joining the ATS in 1945. She appeared in uniform with her parents at the Victory Celebrations later that year. At eighteen, she was granted her own Arms and personal standard, her own car and had her first Lady-in-Waiting and private secretary.

In peacetime, she became President of the Red Cross and other organisations, and launched the aircraft carrier HMS *Eagle*. Her private life was marked by her engagement and marriage to Prince Philip. Her wedding, one of the first Royal occasions following the War, was a magnificent event. Her dress was designed by Norman Hartnell, her ring was of Welsh gold, and she had her sister as chief bridesmaid. Presents poured in from all over the world. Unlike her mother, who was also married at Westminster Abbey, the Princess forgot to leave her bouquet on the Tomb of the Unknown Warrior, but it was specially sent there the next day. For a while after her wedding she was able to live as a Naval Officer's wife, enjoying a period in Malta while Prince Philip was in command of HMS *Magpie*. But soon her father's ill-health forced her to take on more official duties. In 1952, the King's condition worsened and he died, and Princess Elizabeth became Queen of England at the age of twenty-six.

Left *Princess Elizabeth at the age of seventeen. The picture was taken during the Second World War, in 1943.*
Opposite *A charming study of the Queen, then Princess Elizabeth, before her wedding in 1947. It shows the beautiful wedding dress designed by Norman Hartnell.*

Far left *The young Princess
Elizabeth, almost a year old,
sitting on the knee of her
grandmother, Queen Mary, in
1927. This was the time her
parents went abroad for six
months, and left their daughter
with her grandparents at
Buckingham Palace.*
Left *Queen Elizabeth, the
Queen Mother, relaxing in the
garden of their London home,
145 Piccadilly, with her
daughter Princess Elizabeth and
two of the family corgis. Six
months later the family moved to
Buckingham Palace.*
Below left *King George VI with
his daughters Princess Elizabeth
and Princess Margaret riding in
Windsor Great Park on the
occasion of his elder child's
twelfth birthday.*
Right *The Princess at sixteen
shortly after becoming honorary
Colonel of the Grenadier
Guards. She proudly wears the
regimental badge in her hat.*
Below *Princess Elizabeth as
No 230873 a Junior Subaltern
in the ATS during the Second
World War in 1945.*

7

Far left *A picture of Princess Elizabeth and Prince Philip taken on their engagement in 1947.*

Below far left *Princess Elizabeth and Prince Philip after their wedding on 20th November 1947 in Westminster Abbey. The wedding group includes the King and Queen, Princess Margaret as chief bridesmaid, and other members of the Royal family.*

Left *The band plays 'God Save the Queen', troops present arms and the crowd rises to its feet as the golden State Coach takes Queen Elizabeth II to her Coronation at Westminster Abbey on 2nd June 1953.*

Below centre *A happy scene on Coronation Day 1953, showing the newly-crowned Queen with Prince Philip, Prince Charles and Princess Anne waving from the balcony at Buckingham Palace.*

Below *After her Coronation the Queen and the Duke of Edinburgh drive back to the Palace in the State Coach.*

Opposite *Taken in 1950, this picture shows Princess Elizabeth and the Duke of Edinburgh with Prince Charles and the new baby Princess Anne, who was born at Clarence House.*

Below *A formal portrait of the Queen and Duke of Edinburgh after the Coronation. The Queen, in Robes of State and Crown, is said to have remarked that they were rather heavy to wear.*

Life in Public

As the Queen's life is so busy, every day has to be planned well in advance to ensure the smooth running of all arrangements. Following a tradition begun in the reign of Queen Victoria, a piper plays outside her window every morning at nine o'clock to signal the start of the day's working schedule. Each day the Sovereign must read the contents of the despatch boxes, and she also gives the Prime Minister a regular audience.

Fourteen Investitures are held each year at which Honours conferred in the New Year and Birthday Honours Lists are presented.

On Maundy Thursday the Queen distributes the traditional Maundy Money to selected recipients. The Queen used to carry out this ceremony at Westminster Abbey each year, and it is always attended by the Yeoman Warders. Lately she has visited other Cathedrals, particularly if they have a special anniversary to celebrate.

In May the Queen visits the Chelsea Flower Show in the grounds of the Royal Hospital. June is a busy month for her, beginning with the Annual Ceremony of the Service of the Order of the Garter in St George's Chapel, Windsor. The Queen was installed on 23rd April 1948 (her birthday) as a Lady of the Order, and is now Sovereign of the Order. On her official birthday she rides at the head of her Guards to attend the Trooping the Colour Ceremony on Horse Guards Parade. Following the Trooping the Colour there is Royal Ascot Week, and in July Garden Parties are held in England and Scotland. In November are the annual Remembrance Day Service at the Cenotaph and wreath laying ceremony, the Royal Command Variety Performance and, at the end of the year, the traditional Christmas Day broadcast which is now televised. All these engagements are normal routine, with overseas tours and countless other duties to be fitted in as well.

Ceremonies

Left *The Queen in the House of Lords on 15th May 1979, making her speech outlining the programme of the newly-elected Conservative Government. The Duke of Edinburgh is next to her, Prince Charles is on her left and Princess Anne is on her right.*
Opposite *Her Majesty wearing the Imperial State Crown and her Parliamentary Robe in the throne room of Buckingham Palace in 1977.*

Below *Accompanied by the Duke of Edinburgh, the Queen takes the salute at the Trooping the Colour Ceremony. The ceremony, held to mark the Sovereign's Official Birthday, is* a military parade. The Queen, as Colonel of the Army, reviews the five regiments of Foot Guards and two regiments of mounted Guards.

Opposite above *The Queen and* Duke of Edinburgh leave Buckingham Palace to take part in the annual ceremony of Trooping the Colour.

Opposite below *Trooping the Colour over for another year, the* Queen and her family wave from the balcony of Buckingham Palace. Prince Charles, in the uniform of Colonel-in-Chief of the Welsh Guards, had also taken part in the parade.

Opposite *Preceded by the Governor of the Castle, Military Knights of Windsor, Officers of Arms and Knights of the Garter, the procession winds its way down the slope from Windsor Castle to St George's Chapel for the Annual Service. At the Service, held in June, traditional prayers, for the Order are said, and on duty in the Chapel are the Queen's Bodyguard of Honourable Corps of Gentlemen-at-Arms and the Yeoman of the Guard. Above The Queen and her procession ride in their open landaus to the Garter Ceremony. Left The Queen, who is Sovereign of the Order, wearing the robes of the Order of the Garter.*

Above *At Caernarvon Castle on 1st July 1969, the Queen with Prince Philip, the Queen Mother and Princess Anne arrive for the Investiture of Prince Charles as Prince of Wales. The Prince is in the background as they alight at the station.*

Right *The Queen with Prince Charles listening to the speeches after the Investiture.*

Opposite above *The Queen at the Tower of London with the Governor and Yeoman Warders (usually called Beefeaters) in their Tudor Costume. The ceremonial axe and partisan (or halberd) are in the foreground.*

Opposite below *The Queen, with Prince Philip and family after the funeral service for Lord Louis Mountbatten, held at Westminster Abbey on 5th September 1979.*

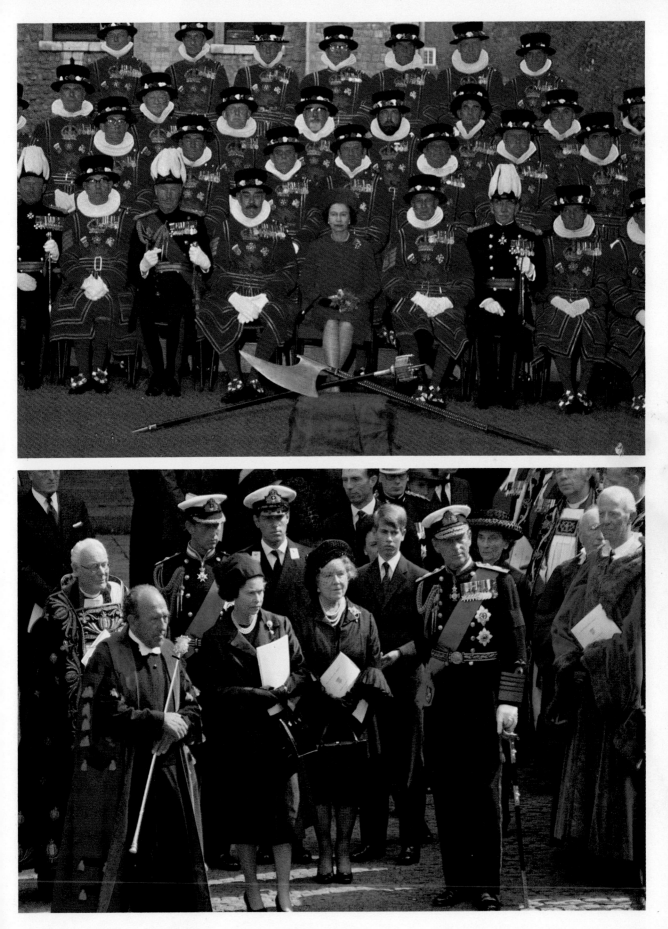

General Royal duties

Left *The Queen with Sir Francis Chichester as he was about to board* Gypsy Moth IV. *She had just knighted him in a public ceremony at the Royal Naval College, Greenwich. It reminded people of the occasion when the first Queen Elizabeth knighted Sir Francis Drake in public.*
Below *The Queen visiting the Argyll and Sutherland Highlanders in barracks at Catterick. She is their Colonel-in-Chief.*

Left *The Queen launches her namesake* Queen Elizabeth II *at John Brown's shipyard, Clydebank on 20th September 1967. This is a general view showing the vessel going down the slipway. Her mother, as Queen Elizabeth, had launched the first* Queen Elizabeth *on the 27th September 1939.*
Below *The Queen with her husband, daughter and sister at a dance at the Palace of Holyroodhouse in Scotland.*

Below *The Queen dancing at the Annual Ghillies' Ball held at Balmoral in 1972. It was the year of the celebration of her Silver Wedding.*

Opposite above *One Royal occasion which the Queen always enjoys. She is seen here taking part in the ceremonial drive up the course at Royal Ascot.*

Opposite below *The Queen conferring the Honorary Degree of Doctor of Music on her mother at the Royal College of Music in December 1973.*

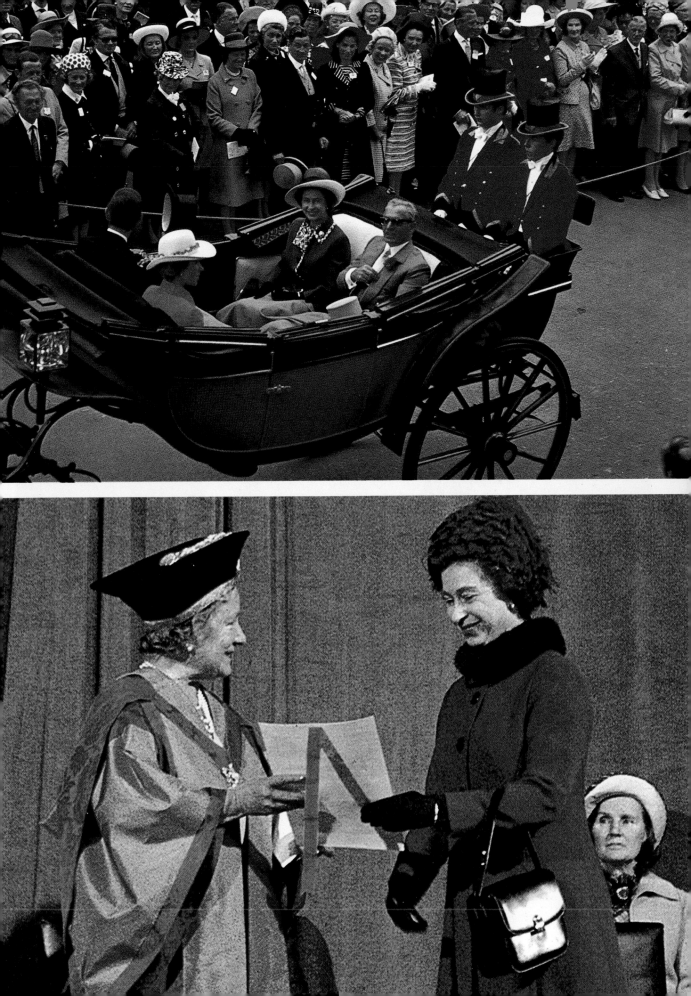

Opposite *The Queen looking immaculate in white overalls, scarf and helmet as she visits a Yorkshire colliery in 1975, accompanied by the Duke of Edinburgh.*
Right *A devoted patron of the Arts, the Queen is seen here talking with members of the cast in costume after an opera performance in 1976.*
Below *The scene at the Royal Garden Party in the grounds of Buckingham Palace in Jubilee year 1977. These popular events, held each summer in July, replace the Presentation Parties and Debutante Balls of other reigns, and enable a vast number of the Queen's subjects to visit Buckingham Palace and sometimes be presented to her.*

Silver Jubilee

Opposite above *Everywhere the Queen went visiting on her Jubilee tours she was presented with flowers. At times there were so many she seemed to be overwhelmed. In this photograph, some of the posies, single flowers and bouquets are piled up in the back of her car.*

Opposite below *In Jubilee Year, 1977, the Queen visited most parts of the British Isles. In this picture she is talking to wellwishers at dockland, wearing, appropriately enough, a 'sailor' hat.*

Above *Enthusiastic crowds clinging on to the railings in order to catch a glimpse of the Queen near Buckingham Palace on Jubilee Day.*

Right *The traditional Spithead Review of the Fleet for the Jubilee in 1977. This is one of the ships dressed 'overall' with sailors lining the decks in review order.*

Above *With Prince Charles in the uniform of Colonel-in-Chief of the Welsh Guards riding behind, the Queen and Duke of Edinburgh ride in the Golden State Coach to the Thanksgiving Service at St Paul's Cathedral in celebration of the Queen's Jubilee in 1977.*

Left *During her Jubilee visit to Northern Ireland, the Queen talked to young people in Ulster.*

Above right *The Queen and Duke of Edinburgh taking part in the Service of Thanksgiving for her Jubilee at St Paul's Cathedral in June 1977.*
Right *The Queen alighting from her helicopter at the start of her visit to Belfast in 1977. The Right Hon. Roy Mason MP, then Secretary of State for Northern Ireland is immediately behind her.*

Above *The Queen and her family acknowledging the cheers of the crowds from the balcony of Buckingham Palace on Jubilee Day 1977.*

Far left *These attractive bookmarks and drink mats were two of the souvenirs produced to commemorate the Silver Jubilee.*

Centre left *Two more of the many commemorative souvenirs of the Jubilee.*

Left *A special commemorative beaker bearing the Royal Arms to celebrate the Silver Jubilee.*

The Queen as Ambassador

The Queen's role as a diplomat began early in her reign, for, on 19th February 1952, thirteen days after her Accession, she received the German Chancellor, Dr Adenauer, in audience. In the 1950s relations between Britain and Germany were re-established and the first German Ambassador since the Second World War was received by the Queen in 1955.

Each year two or three State Visitors are welcomed to England, entertained in London and, increasingly, at Windsor. Germany, Italy and France have sent two Presidents and Sweden two Kings. Of course, the Queen is related to many foreign monarchs so their visits have personal as well as official significance.

When travelling abroad, the Queen flies in an aircraft of the Queen's Flight or *Concorde*. At sea, the Royal Yacht *Britannia*, which was launched in 1954, is used as a floating residence for the Queen. On board she can entertain her guests or relax with her family.

In 1951 Princess Elizabeth had a private audience with Pope Pius III, but in 1961 she made a State Visit to the Vatican as Queen to meet another Head of Church, Pope John.

In 1953 and 1954 the Queen and Duke of Edinburgh undertook a very long tour of the Commonwealth. On that tour she was the first reigning monarch to visit New Zealand, and she also went to Bermuda, Jamaica, Fiji, Tonga, Sri Lanka (then Ceylon), Australia, Uganda, Malta and Gibraltar.

One of the highlights of her tour to India in 1961 was her ride on the back of an elephant. Four years later, in 1965 she visited Germany, the first British Sovereign to do so for fifty-two years, and in May 1978 went on a five-day tour of West Germany. In Jubilee Year, 1977, she made another long tour of the Commonwealth countries and in 1979 she paid an official visit to the Middle East. Here, strict observance of Moslem Laws had to be observed, and the sight of a woman holding a position of such authority was entirely new to these people.

As Ambassador at home

Left *The Queen driving in an open landau with Yang Di Pertuan Agong of Malaysia during his official visit to England.*
Opposite *The Queen with King Gustav of Sweden during his State Visit to England.*

Right *Wearing a tiara and Order of the Garter, the Queen greets King Faisal during his visit to England.*

Below *The Queen, Prince Philip, Queen Elizabeth the Queen Mother, the Duke and Duchess of Kent, Prince Charles and Princess Anne with the Japanese Emperor Hirohito and the Empress Nageko, at Buckingham Palace in October 1971. The Emperor is seen wearing the Order of the Garter, which was removed during the Second World War and only restored to him a few months before his visit.*

As Ambassador abroad

Opposite *The Queen in a howdah riding on an elephant during her visit to the sacred city of Benares in February 1961. From her high perch she was able to look out over the great crowds of people who came to see her.*

Above *One of the Queen's most colourful and memorable tours was in India in 1961. Here she is in New Delhi watching a display of dancing by Girl Guides, wearing national costume rather than uniform.*
Left *The Queen and Duke of Edinburgh visiting the Taj Mahal at Agra in January 1961. The Queen looked at her reflection in daylight and came back at night to see it again by moonlight!*
Opposite above *The Royal Yacht* Britannia *coming into harbour with its usual welcoming escort of little ships.*
Opposite below *In 1972, the Queen visited the island of Mauritius. On this tour she journeyed some 25,000 miles. She is said to be the world's most travelled woman.*

Opposite above *In 1972, the Queen visited the Communist country of Yugoslavia. Here she is seen with Princess Anne during her tour.*

Opposite below *A Maori welcome in New Zealand. The Queen is wearing the traditional Maori cloak.*

Below *In 1973, the Queen visited Canada twice. Here she is seen walking outside against the background of a crowd on one of her trips.*

Left *The Queen pictured in 1974 with the former Canadian Prime Minister, Pierre Trudeau, on one of her 'walkabouts', meeting and talking with the people in the streets.*

Below *In Hong Kong in 1975, the Queen dotting the eye of a dragon. Once the eyes are dotted, the dragon is said to be alive and able to take part in a colourful procession.*

Opposite *The Queen making friends with children at a swimming pool in Kowloon in May 1975. She is herself an excellent swimmer, so, in the heat, she may have envied them their swim.*

Above *In 1977, the Queen paid a private visit to the Island of Mustique where her sister Princess Margaret has a home. Here they are walking together and enjoying the sunshine, with the Duke of Edinburgh just behind.*

Left *The Queen and Duke of Edinburgh on a recent visit to Tanzania with Prince Andrew.*

Opposite *In 1976, the Queen and Duke went to America to join in the Bicentennial celebrations. Here she is in Washington, dancing with President Ford.*

Above *In 1976, the Queen and Duke of Edinburgh paid a visit to Wall Street, New York to see the world of American commerce.*

Right *An official reception at which the Queen, accompanied by President Ford, watches the march past of a colourful band, with a guard of honour formed by armed services.*

Opposite above *The Queen in Boston admiring an enormous cake made in her honour and iced in blue and white. The main decoration was a model of the Royal Yacht* Britannia.

Opposite below *Pictured stepping off Concorde on her arrival in Barbados in 1977, the Queen begins another visit.*

45

Left *The Queen talking to a group of children in Barbados during her visit in Jubilee Year, 1977.*
Above *Another visit to Australia in 1977. The Queen in Sydney with the famous Sydney Harbour bridge and Opera House in the background.*
Right *Prince Philip takes the salute at a march past in Australia. The Queen is at his side in Court dress, with tiara.*

Above *In 1965, the Queen was the first British monarch to go to West Germany since 1913. Here she is inspecting a guard of honour on her arrival in 1979.*
Right *The Queen and Prince Philip alighting from Concorde and being welcomed at Riyadh Airport in Saudi Arabia in 1979. In deference to Moslem custom, the Queen wore a long sapphire blue dress for the occasion. She was the first reigning British monarch to set foot on Arab soil.*

Above *Accompanied by the Foreign Secretary, Dr David Owen, MP, the Queen talks to Sheikh Jabir, the Crown Prince of Kuwait.*
Right *The Queen and Duke of Edinburgh with their Arab hosts at the Meriden Hotel in Abu Dhabi in 1979. The visit of a woman Head of State, though unusual to the people of a Moslem country, was a resounding success.*

Private Life

Queen Elizabeth II is very close to all the members of her family and takes great delight in her children who, despite the difference in their ages, are very united. Remembering her own experiences as a child when she was groomed for monarchy by her father, the Queen shares many of her duties with Prince Charles.

She has a very real love of animals, particularly horses and dogs. Learning to ride at the age of three, she was able to teach her own children herself, and is particularly proud of Princess Anne who has won International recognition in Three Day Events and represented England in the Montreal Olympic Games. Prince Charles, like Prince Philip, is a polo player of renown. His father, has now given up the game because of an injury but has taken up the sport of driving at which he excels.

One of the Queen's favourite pastimes is her interest in horse racing and she is acknowledged as an authority on owning and breeding race-horses. They have won hundreds of Classics on the flat, her first Classic Winner being Pall Mall in the Two Thousand Guineas at Newmarket,

but none of them has ever won a Derby. At one time she also raced steeplechasers but after the death of her horse, Manicou, she concentrated on flat racing. One of her wedding presents was a filly, Astrakhan, given to her by the Aga Khan. The Queen also breeds Event horses, notably Doublet and Columbus ridden by Princess Anne, carriage horses and polo and Fell and Highland ponies. She takes a great interest in all her stock, visiting them regularly in training.

Her reign has been an eventful one, highlighted by Prince Charles' Investiture in 1969, her daughter's wedding in 1973, her own Silver Wedding in 1972 and her Silver Jubilee in 1977. The Queen spends much of her time at Buckingham Palace in London, but she enjoys weekends at Windsor Castle, her long summer holiday in Balmoral and her visit to Sandringham in Norfolk after Christmas.

The Queen's Jubilee Year, 1977, was notable for another happy event – the birth of her first grandson, Peter Phillips.

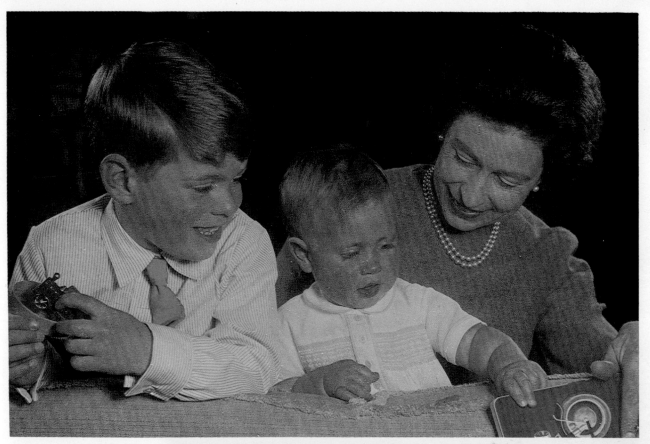

Opposite *Taken in 1959, the Queen in jodhpurs with Princess Anne at Windsor. The Princess is busy playing with a boat, while her mother holds the tow rope.*

Above *The Queen with her two younger sons, Prince Andrew and Prince Edward.*

Right *An informal picture of the Royal family at Windsor, with the Royal Lodge in the background. Prince Charles is trying to make the young Prince Edward laugh at the camera.*

Left *This picture was taken in 1969 for the film* Royal Family *and shows the Queen, the Duke of Edinburgh, Prince Charles and Princess Anne enjoying an informal meal at Windsor.*
Below *Another informal study of the Queen and her family enjoying the sunshine at Windsor.*
Opposite *Princess Anne's wedding to Captain Mark Phillips took place at Westminster Abbey on 14th November 1973 – Prince Charles' twenty-fifth birthday. The nine-year-old Prince Edward was a page and held his sister's train.*

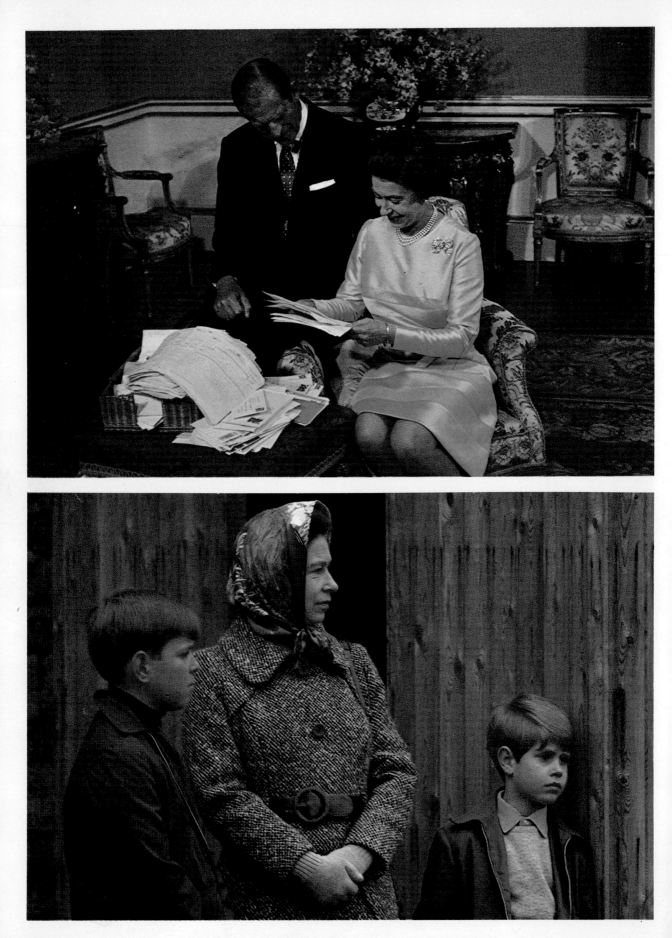

Opposite above *The Queen and Prince Philip smiling over some of the many congratulatory messages they received on the occasion of their Silver Wedding in 1972.*

Opposite below *An informal study of the Queen with Prince Andrew and Prince Edward.*

Below *Her Majesty, a very intent spectator at the Badminton Horse Trials. This event, which takes place in April each year, is a regular favourite with members of the Royal family. Princess Anne participates frequently with her husband Captain Mark Phillips, and Prince Charles has acted as steward.*

Opposite above *The Queen, with Prince Philip, Prince Charles and Princess Anne sharing a relaxed moment on board the Royal Yacht Britannia during their tour of Australia.*

Opposite below *The Queen talking with her Private Secretary Sir Martin Charteris on board the Royal Yacht Britannia in 1972.*

Below *A laughing Queen on the deck of the Royal Yacht Britannia.*

Above *The Queen and Prince Philip on the rail of the Royal Yacht* Britannia *in 1972.*
Right *A delightful study of the Queen at Balmoral with four of her black labradors.*
Opposite *The Queen riding at Balmoral in 1972. From her vantage point she looks back and points out the Castle.*

Left *A Brigade of Guards band with drum major at the head, marching out of Windsor Castle.* Below *Balmoral Castle on Deeside in the heart of the highlands. It was purchased by Queen Victoria in 1842 and enlarged and is said to be the Royal family's favourite holiday home. They spend each summer there, enjoying such Scottish pursuits as stalking, walking, shooting, sailing and fishing.*

Above *Sandringham House in Norfolk which has been the private possession of the Royal family since the reign of Edward VII. It is surrounded by a vast area of land which provides excellent shooting for the Duke of Edinburgh and Prince Charles. The Royal stud is also there. Normally the family stay at Sandringham for a short time after spending Christmas at Windsor Castle.*

Left *Buckingham Palace, the official London home of the Queen and her family. It was originally built in 1702 by the Duke of Buckingham and named after him. George III purchased it, renaming it Queen's House in honour of his wife, but its old name was given back to it by Queen Victoria who refurbished it.*

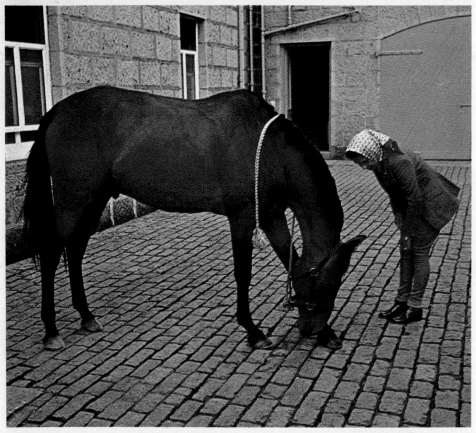

Above *A charming family group
taken at Balmoral for the
Queen's thirty-second wedding
anniversary. Princess Anne is
holding the hand of Peter
Phillips, the Queen's first
grandson, now aged two. He
seems to be following the family
tradition and growing fast!*
Left *The Queen with one of her
horses at Balmoral after a
morning ride.*
Opposite *A charming study of
the Queen at Balmoral in 1972,
sitting by a splashing waterfall,
with two of her corgis at her side.*

*The Queen and Prince Philip in
an informal picture taken by
Patrick Lichfield in 1972 for
their Silver Wedding.*

Acknowledgements

The publishers would like to thank the following for their help in
supplying photographs for this book.

All photographs are by courtesy of Camera Press Limited except
those listed below:

Colour Library International: page 15 (bottom).

Keystone Press Agency Limited: page 19 (bottom), page 25
(top).

Popperfoto: page 6 (bottom), page 8 (top), page 35, page 53.

The Press Association Limited: page 12, page 20 (top), page 21
(top), page 62 (top).

First English edition published 1980 by
Intercontinental Book Productions, Berkshire House,
Queen Street, Maidenhead, Berkshire, England

Copyright © MCMLXXX by Intercontinental Book Productions
All rights reserved

This edition is published by Crescent Books, a division of Crown
Publishers, Inc, by arrangement with Intercontinental Book
Productions

A B C D E F G H
Printed in Hong Kong

Library of Congress Cataloging in Publication Data

Leete-Hodge, Lornie.
  The Queen.

  1. Elizabeth II, Queen of Great Britain, 1926 –
Iconography. 2. Great Britain – Kings and rulers –
Iconography. I. Title.
DA590.L4   1980   941.085'092'4 [B]   79-26619
ISBN 0-517-30811-8